15 HOUR WORD PROCESSING
USING THE BBC MICRO

WITH WORDWISE and WORDWISE PLUS

Anna Ruthven

National Extension College

Anna Ruthven is an experienced lecturer who has taught secretarial and business studies at Polytechnic, Further Education and School levels in Britain and Australia.

ISBN 0 86082 686 4
Published by The National Extension College Trust Ltd, 18 Brooklands Avenue, Cambridge CB2 2HN.
Printed by NEC Print
Cover design: Robert Ruthven

Contents

Advanced features

Introduction

Welcome to *15 Hour Word Processing Using the BBC Micro with WORDWISE and WORDWISE PLUS.*

This book is aimed at:

- the student who is on a short course
- the student who only has a limited number of hours available for 'hands on' experience
- the student who wishes to use the book as an introduction to word processing with WORDWISE and WORDWISE PLUS.

The first half of the course concentrates on learning and using various command/function keys. The later sections build and expand on the skills learnt and follow the theme of working in a Personnel Office.

The book is self-pacing and self-teaching. If you only have time to complete the Elementary Section then you should gain a basic understanding of word processing. If, however, you do have time to complete all sections, then you will have carried out several of the major aspects of the wp operator.

At the end of the book you will find the Help Index — if you have forgotten a command sequence all you have to do is look it up in the Help Index.

You will also find at the end of the book the Key to Exercises — once you have worked through a section, check your version against the one in the Key to Exercises. There is additional material at the end of each section with ideas for further practice.

ORDER FORM

Title	No.	Cost
15 Hour Word Processing Using the BBC Micro with View @ £4.95	. . . . . .	. . . . . .
15 Hour Word Processing Using the BBC Micro with Wordwise and Wordwise Plus @ £4.95	. . . . . .	. . . . . .
15 Hour Word Processing Using the Amstrad Word Processor @ £5.95	. . . . . .	. . . . . .
15 Hour Word Processing Using WordStar @ £5.95	. . . . . .	. . . . . .
Word Processing Practical Exercises @ £4.95	. . . . . .	. . . . . .

Discount available for bulk purchasers.

I enclose a cheque for £. . . . . (we can only invoice orders of a minimum value of £10 sent with an official order form).

Name. . . . .

Address. . . . .

. . . .

National Extension College, 18 Brooklands Avenue, Cambridge CB2 2HN. Phone: (0223) 316644

☐ Tick here if you would like us to send you details about our forthcoming title *Wordprocessing: the trainer's manual* by Anna Ruthven.

Elementary features

Section 1

1.1 Getting started

In order to complete this course you will need to have a:

- BBC 'B' Microcomputer fitted with the WORDWISE or WORDWISE PLUS word processing system
- Disk Drive
- Visual Display Unit (VDU)
- Keyboard with the Wordwise Prompt Card in place (ie, Insert or Over Command should be lined up with the red function key **f0**).
- Printer.

1   Make sure your machine has been switched on.

2   Take your disk out of its envelope: make sure that you handle it with *care* and *do not touch* the exposed area of the disk. Now with the label uppermost and nearest to you gently place the disk in your disk drive and close the disk drive door.

3   Now turn your attention to your screen and keyboard. To move into WORDWISE carry out the following steps:

START-UP PROCEDURE

TYPE: *W.

PRESS: RETURN

```
BBC Computer

Acorn DFS

BASIC

>*W._
```

Photo 1 shows the screen in BASIC with *W. typed in.

1

You are now in WORDWISE — or WORDWISE PLUS — and ready to start word processing. If nothing happens then PRESS: `BREAK` and TYPE: *W. again and make sure you have put the point in and pressed `RETURN` . *NOTE:* you must PRESS: `RETURN` at the end of each command or it will not work. You can type commands with `CAPS LOCK` on (ie, in capital letters) but you must not have the `SHIFT LOCK` on. To move into Edit Mode, WORDWISE PLUS users just PRESS: `ESCAPE` . WORDWISE users will then see a question on the screen asking if you want the old text or not. As you do not have any text typed in yet, PRESS: N.

You will now be in **Menu Mode** and at the moment all you want to do is type. To move into the mode for typing, the **Edit Mode**, PRESS: `ESCAPE` .

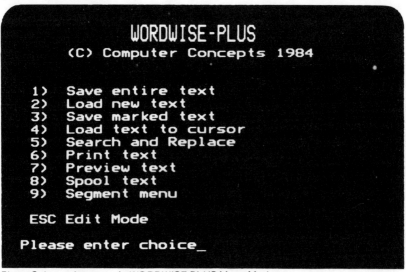

Photo 2 shows the screen in WORDWISE PLUS Menu Mode.

1.2 Status line

In Edit Mode you will notice the **status line** at the top of your screen. The left side is a 'word count' — so you know how many words you have typed, the 'characters free count' shows you how much memory space you have available and at the far right the 'I' means that you are in **Insert Mode**.

Words-0   Characters free-24068 I

Start
-
End

Photo 3 shows the screen in Edit Mode with the Status Line.

If the status line appears to have gone off the top of the screen, return to Menu Mode: PRESS : ESCAPE , and TYPE : *TV 255, Ø and PRESS : RETURN . Then return to Edit Mode (PRESS : ESCAPE) and the status line should now be visible.

1.3 Cursor

Notice the flashing line beneath 'START' — this flashing line is your cursor.

1.4 Wrap-around

The system is a wrap-around system which means that when you are typing you do not have to press RETURN at the end of the line: the system will automatically move your cursor down to the next line. You only press RETURN at the end of a paragraph — when you turn up 2 line spaces (ie, PRESS : RETURN twice). One of the effects of wrap-around is that sometimes a space occurs at the left hand margin — don't worry if this happens there will not be a space there on printing.

3

1.5 Setting left margin

Ready to get started? Set your left hand margin first. To do this: PRESS : red function key **f1** — this gives the system an **embedded command** (ie, one you cannot see as it is embedded in the system) and TYPE: **LM1Ø** and then PRESS: red function key **f2** to tell the system that you have ended your embedded command.
NOTE: you must *ALWAYS* press the START EMBEDDED COMMAND, red function key **f1** , when you want to use an embedded command and you must press the END EMBEDDED COMMAND, red function key **f2** , when you finish your embedded command.

Now just to go over what you have done: you should have pressed **f1** , typed **LM1Ø** and pressed **f2** . You have now set your left margin at 10. (The 'code' for left margin is LM.)

1.6 Setting the line length

Now with your cursor still on the same line as your first embedded command, give a second embedded command, this time to set the length of your typing line. PRESS : **f1** TYPE: **LL6Ø** PRESS : **f2** . You have now set your line length at 60 character spaces (the 'code' for line length is LL). The left margin and line length that you have set are fine with continuous stationery. However, if you are using A4 sheets you might want to set a wider left margin, or longer line length.

1.7 Right hand margin justification

Finally, still with your cursor on the same line, give an embedded command to have your right hand margin justified — like this book. PRESS: **f1** TYPE : **JO** PRESS : **f2** . You have now turned the justification on ('code' JO) and you are ready to start typing.

Photo 4 shows the screen in Edit Mode with the commands for setting the left margin, line length and justification.

If you have your **CAPS LOCK** red light on, cancel it by pressing **CAPS LOCK** again.

Please copy type 1.8 below. Don't worry if you make any typing errors, as you will correct them at the end.

1.8

Using your Electric or Manual typewriter, how fast can you type? Thirty or forty words a minute, maybe sixty? Invariably your speed will slow down when working on production tasks, particularly if you have to stop to correct your errors. One of the many good things about word processing is that correcting errors has never been easier, whether it's just a small typing error or inserting a word, perhaps a whole line – or even a paragraph.

Your speed and confidence should therefore grow with the more word processing you do and we are starting right here!

1.9 Cursor control

Finished typing? Made any errors? If not then type an extra line in — with some errors!

Now you will have noticed that as you were typing the cursor moved along with the text. It is important that you know how to move your cursor around your text as quickly as possible. Try out the following manoeuvre with your cursor: use the arrow keys on the right of the keyboard to move your cursor around the screen.

There are some quicker ways to move the cursor in conjunction with the **SHIFT** key. With **SHIFT LOCK** on, press the 'up' arrow key **↑** , — your cursor should fly up to the top of your text. Now press the 'down' arrow key **↓** and the cursor will move to the end of your text. The horizontal arrow keys **→** **←** when used in conjunction with the **SHIFT** will move the cursor to the beginning or end of the line.

Cancel your **SHIFT LOCK** before continuing — to cancel it you just press it again.

Now for your corrections and the alterations I want you to make to the text (see 1.10 which follows). *PLEASE READ THE INSTRUCTIONS IN 1.11 — 1.16 BEFORE ATTEMPTING TO CORRECT YOUR ERRORS!*

1.10

[Key to correction marks: When a letter is underlined it means you have to change it. Look at the instruction in the margin. *l/c* means lower case, i.e. small letter, and *u/c* means upper case, i.e. capital letter. For example Electric/ *l c* would be changed to electric and your/*u c* would be changed to Your.]

l/c Using your Electric or Manual typewriter, how fast can you type?

Thirty or forty words a minute, maybe sixty? ~~Invariably~~ your *u/c*

speed will slow down when working on production tasks,

particularly if you have to stop to correct your errors. One of the

many good ~~things~~ *Points* about ~~word processing~~ *this system* is that correcting errors

has never been easier, whether it's just a small typing error or

inserting a *missing* word, perhaps a whole line — or even a paragraph.

Your speed and confidence ~~should therefore~~ *will* grow with the more word processing you do. ~~and we are starting right here~~!

1.11 Inserting

Ready to correct and edit your work?

It is easy to insert missing characters, words or spaces as you are in Insert Mode (see the 'I' at the top right hand side of your status line). All you have to do is place your cursor where the missing character or word is — and type it in. The text will move to the right to accommodate the new character or word.

To replace characters, or overwrite characters you need to be in **Over Mode.** PRESS : red function key 【f0】 and you will see that an 'O' has now appeared at the top right hand side of your status line. In this mode you can 'overtype' by just placing your cursor under the character you need to correct and then typing in the correct character.

REMEMBER TO RETURN TO INSERT MODE — PRESS : red function key 【f0】 again. You will see 'I' reappear on your status line.

1.12 Deleting

To delete characters, PRESS : **CTRL** (Control) and the **A** key at the same time. Place your cursor under the character you want to delete and just PRESS : **CTRL** and **A** . If you hold **CTRL** and A down characters will continue to be deleted to the right of your cursor. You can also use **CTRL** and **A** to link up lines when you have unnecessary gaps — as **CTRL** and **A** delete spaces as well as characters.

There is also a black **DELETE** key at the bottom right hand side of your keyboard: this deletes characters to the left of the cursor.

To delete a word, place your cursor under the word to be deleted and PRESS : **CTRL** and the **D** key at the same time.

To change characters or words from upper to lower case, or vice versa, place your cursor under the character you want to change and PRESS : **CTRL** and the **S** key.

You will notice that in the text alterations you are asked to delete the last few words '. . . and we are starting right here!' To do this bring your cursor to the space after the word 'do' and then PRESS : red function key **f6** DELETE TO? You will notice at the top of your screen the question DELETE TO? appears. The system needs to know where the deletion is to end. You want it to end where the exclamation mark is so TYPE : ! and everything to the right of the cursor up to the exclamation mark will be deleted. Now delete the exclamation mark with **CTRL** and **A**.

To insert a line, PRESS : **RETURN**

Now having read the instructions, go ahead and make all the necessary corrections.

All corrections made?

1.13 Previewing text (Option 7)

I expect you would like to see what your text would look like in its **formatted** (or finished) state with the 60 space typing line and the right hand margin justified. To do this, PRESS : **ESCAPE** and you will be in Menu Mode. (Don't worry you won't lose your text in Edit Mode.) Choose number 7 from the Menu list – the one called PREVIEW TEXT. PRESS : 7 and immediately the screen begins to 'scroll' your text in its formatted state. If the screen moves too fast for you, WORDWISE users PRESS : **CTRL** and **SHIFT** together. WORDWISE PLUS users PRESS : your space bar once to stop scrolling – press it again to restart scrolling.

1.14 Merging

Before moving back into Edit Mode make a note of any corrections you want to make to the text. Then move back into Edit Mode in order to make them.

To put an extra line space between paragraphs use the **RETURN** key to insert a line space.

You may have large spaces in sentences which you want to close up: use the **CTRL** and **A** key to link up lines and close up spaces.

1.15 Deleting marked text

Finally, back in Edit Mode move your cursor to the final paragraph and delete it! To do this, place your cursor under the 'Y' of 'Your' and PRESS : MARKER, that's red function key **f3** . Now move your cursor to the space at the end of the paragraph and PRESS : **f3** again. (You will notice two blocks appear on the far right of the status line, showing that you have markers set.) Now PRESS: DELETE MARKED TEXT, red function key **f7** – and that's the end of that paragraph and Section 1!

Check your final version against the one on page 80.

PRESS : **ESCAPE** to move back into Menu Mode. Make sure you are feeling confident with the commands you have learnt.

1.16 Clearing text from screen

How WORDWISE users clear text from Edit Mode:

Either move into Menu Mode and TYPE :*W. PRESS : RETURN and answer 'N' to the question: OLD TEXT OR NOT? *or* PRESS : **BREAK** (black key next to red function key **f9**) and then answer 'N' to the question: OLD TEXT OR NOT?

How WORDWISE PLUS users clear text from Edit Mode:

In Edit Mode place your cursor at the end of the passage (PRESS : **SHIFT** and ↓ at the same time). TYPE : **#** (or another similarly obscure character which is not actually part of your text!) Move your cursor to the top of your passage (PRESS : **SHIFT** and ↑ at the same time). PRESS : red function key **f6** DELETE TO? TYPE : **#** (or whatever obscure character you used) and your screen will be cleared.

1.17 Closing down the system

Should you want to switch off the computer, you should first remove any disk that you might have in the disk drive and then turn off the disk drive, printer, computer and VDU.

An additional exercise follows if you would like further practice before starting the next section. Just type in the exercise and make any corrections or alterations using the commands learnt so far.

Additional material – exercise 1

Copy type the following, make corrections and alter the text using the commands learnt.

POSTAL SERVICES

The Post Office provides an excellent advisory service to business through their Postal Sales Representatives.

These representatives give advice on various postal services, particularly to firms who send out large quantities of mail. Some of these special services include:

Bulk Rebate System, Postage Paid Impressions, Private Boxes, Selectapost and Mail Collection Directly from the Firm.

These services are not just for large firms. Small firms may also benefit from some of the business services offered by the Post Office in particular first-time users of the Business Reply Service, Freepost or Direct Mail Advertising may find that they are entitled to special concessions.

Businesses, large or small, requiring further information on these services should contact the Postal Sales Representative at their main Post Office.

Section 2

You will notice that throughout these exercises I suggest a justified right hand margin. However, if you do not like justified text — leave out the embedded command JO and your text will have a ragged right hand margin similar to normal typewritten text.

TYPE : *W

PRESS : **RETURN**

(WORDWISE users — OLD TEXT OR NOT? will appear on your screen. TYPE : N)

PRESS : **ESCAPE** to move into Edit Mode.

2.1 Setting margin and line length

Set your left margin, your line length and turn the justification on. Do you remember how to do this? PRESS: START EMBEDDED COMMAND **f1** and TYPE: LM1Ø (or whatever left hand margin that you want to set) then PRESS : END EMBEDDED COMMAND **f2** . Now on the same line, PRESS : **f1** TYPE : LL6Ø (or whatever line length you want to set) PRESS: **f2** and finally PRESS : **f1** TYPE : JO and PRESS : **f2** .

NOTE: embedded commands will not take effect if you have your **SHIFT LOCK** on. It is perfectly all right though to have your **CAPS LOCK** on.

You are now ready to copy type Section 2.2.

2.2

To become self-employed is the aim of many people but actually setting up in business is a daunting prospect. Where to start?

First of all the prospective entrepreneur must decide on the type of business she or he will establish and ask themself is there really a

11

market for my product? If the answer is yes then they need to decide whether they will be a sole trader or go into partnership, form a company, perhaps with limited liability, or join with like-minded people in a co-operative venture.

There are various Government initiatives to help the small business to flourish and it is important that the prospective entrepreneur should be aware of the help available.

Finance is, of course, of great importance and a good bank manager is essential — not only for financial advice but also for general business advice.

Finished typing? PRESS : **RETURN** twice before continuing — this is because you will be moving the last paragraph later and an extra couple of line spaces will be needed.
    Now move your cursor to the top of your text (ie, PRESS : **SHIFT** and **↑** at the same time). Proof read your work through for any errors, using the appropriate keys to make corrections. A review of the keys already learnt for correcting and editing text follows.

CTRL and **A** pressed together delete the character above the cursor and, if held down, characters to the right of the cursor. With this combination you can also delete spaces and link up lines.

CTRL and **D** pressed together will delete the word above the cursor.

CTRL and **S** pressed together will change the case of characters.

DELETE key deletes the character to the left of the cursor.

Insert Mode, the mode you should be in, allows you to insert missing characters, spaces or words.

Over Mode: to overwrite characters, PRESS: red function key **f0** . Remember to return to Insert Mode when you have completed your overwriting, PRESS : **f0** again.

RETURN   inserts a line space.

DELETE TO?, red function key **f6** , deletes the line from the cursor up to a specified character.

DELETE MARKED TEXT, red function key **f7** is used in conjunction with MARKER, red function key **f3** . Set a marker at the beginning and end of the piece to be deleted and then PRESS : DELETE MARKED TEXT.

Section 2.3 follows with further text editing for you. There are some new commands here so please do read the instructions in 2.4 and 2.5 before attempting the editing.

2.3

To become self-employed is the aim of many people ~~but actually~~ *and*

N.P. setting up in business ~~is a daunting prospect.~~ *can change your life* /Where to start?

you as

First of all the prospective entrepreneur must decide on the type

you

of business ~~she or he~~ will establish and ask ~~them~~self *your* is there really

v|c a market for my product? If the answer is yes then ~~they~~ *you* need to

you

decide whether ~~they~~ will be a sole trader or go into partnership, *or*

form a company, perhaps with limited liability, or join with like-minded people in a co-operative venture.

* (*Insert final block of text here*)

There are various Government initiatives to help the small business ~~to flourish~~ and it is important that ~~the~~ *you* ~~prospective entrepreneur~~

13

should be aware of the help available.

move this block of text and insert at : ✳

Finance is, of course, of great importance and a good bank manager is essential — not only for financial advice but also for general business advice.

2.4 Text editing

Check: Are you in Insert Mode? 'I' should be displayed on the status line. Look at the text editing asked for in the first paragraph. You should be able to manage the inserting, overwriting, changing case and deleting which you have already learnt. But in order to put 'Where to start?' on to a separate line place your cursor under the space before the 'W' of 'Where' and PRESS : **RETURN** . The sentence will be moved down to the next line. In order to separate this line from the first paragraph you must now insert an extra line. To do this, place your cursor under the 'W' of 'Where' and PRESS : **RETURN** again.

2.5 Moving marked text

In order to swap the last two paragraphs around — place your cursor under the 'F' of 'Finance' (the word which starts the last paragraph) and PRESS : MARKER, **f3** . Now move your cursor to the space at the end of the paragraph and set another marker, PRESS : **f3** . Now move your cursor to the place you want the paragraph to be moved to and then PRESS : MOVE MARKED TEXT, red function key **f8** .

When you have finished text editing check your final version against the one on page 81, then move into Menu Mode (by pressing **ESCAPE**).

2.6 Previewing text

If you would like to **preview** your text, PRESS : 7 and your text will be scrolled in its formatted state. Remember if it flashes by too quickly WORDWISE users PRESS : CTRL and SHIFT together and scrolling will stop. WORDWISE PLUS users PRESS : your space bar once to stop scrolling — PRESS: it again to restart scrolling.

2.7 Saving work on to disk (Option 1)

Happy with your text? You are going to save this lesson on to disk. To save work you must be in Menu Mode and you must have a disk in your disk drive.

Look at the options offered on the Menu. This time opt for: 1) SAVE ENTIRE TEXT. PRESS : 1   You will be asked to give your file a name. Call it S2 (followed by your initials). A filename must not contain any spaces or be longer than 7 characters. When you have named your file, PRESS: RETURN and you will see a red light appear on your disk drive to show that your file is being saved on to disk.

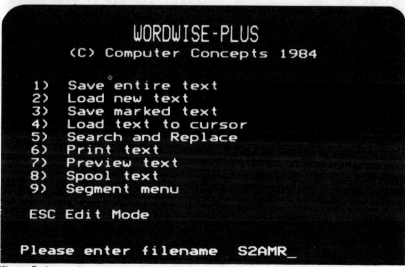

```
              WORDWISE-PLUS
      (C) Computer Concepts 1984

     1)   Save entire text
     2)   Load new text
     3)   Save marked text
     4)   Load text to cursor
     5)   Search and Replace
     6)   Print text
     7)   Preview text
     8)   Spool text
     9)   Segment menu

     ESC Edit Mode

  Please enter filename  S2AMR_
```

Photo 5 shows the screen in Menu Mode, having chosen Option 1, ready to save file S2AMR.

2.8 * CAT

If you want to see if your file has been saved on the disk, check the **disk catalogue**. In Menu Mode, TYPE :*CAT and PRESS : RETURN . A catalogue of files saved on to the disk will be displayed on your screen — your filename should be there!

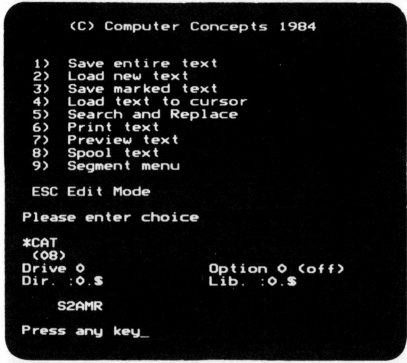

```
        (C) Computer Concepts 1984

    1)   Save entire text
    2)   Load new text
    3)   Save marked text
    4)   Load text to cursor
    5)   Search and Replace
    6)   Print text
    7)   Preview text
    8)   Spool text
    9)   Segment menu

   ESC Edit Mode

   Please enter choice

   *CAT
    (08)
   Drive 0              Option 0 (off)
   Dir. :0.$            Lib. :0.$

        S2AMR

   Press any key_
```

Photo 6 shows the screen in Menu Mode after the Command: *CAT (RETURN).

An additional exercise follows if you would like further practice before starting the next section. Just type in the exercise and make any corrections or alterations using the commands learnt so far.

Additional material – exercise 2

In this passage you will need to use the pound sign – £. If you are using an Epson printer the pound sign will not print out unless you give a special embedded command to define the pound sign: the code is DP35. So, you will PRESS: **f1** TYPE : DP35 and then PRESS : **f2** .

Copy type, correct and edit using the commands learnt.

ENTERPRISE ALLOWANCE SCHEME

Of the many schemes and incentives offered to those wishing to become self-employed, one of the more interesting ones is the Enterprise Allowance Scheme (or EAS).

The EAS is aimed at the unemployed person who wishes to create a new small business. The scheme offers an allowance of £40 a week which takes the place of unemployment or supplementary benefit for 12 months while the business is being established.

To be eligible for the EAS an unemployed person must meet several requirements, the major ones being that she, or he, must be at least 18 and be prepared to work full-time in their business venture. They must have been unemployed for 8 weeks and be in receipt of benefit at the time of applying for the allowance and last, but by no means least, they must show that they have a set amount of money, presently £1,000, to invest in their business.

This scheme is operated by the Manpower Services Commission (MSC) and information is available through local Job Centres.

Section 3

3.1 Recalling a file (Option 2)

Having saved your file on to disk in the last lesson, you are now going to bring it back into the memory and display it on screen in Edit Mode ready for revision.

In Menu Mode look at the options available. You want to load text, which is option 2.

PRESS :   2

You will be asked the name of the file.

TYPE : S2 (followed by your initials)

PRESS :   **RETURN**

As soon as the red light has switched-off on your disk drive then your file should be on display in Edit Mode.

PRESS : **ESCAPE**   to move into Edit Mode.

The updating required for this passage is as follows:

3.2 Inserting a heading

To insert the heading you need to create a line space. Place your cursor under the 'T' of 'To' at the top of the passage and

PRESS : **RETURN**

Move your cursor to the space that has now been created and:

TYPE : **BECOMING SELF-EMPLOYED**

PRESS : **RETURN**

Make sure you have a clear line of space between the heading and the passage.

3.3 Underscoring a heading

(The following are the commands for an Epson printer. If you are using another printer consult the printer manual.)

WORDWISE users: to underscore using WORDWISE, you use a printer command and you will not see the underscore when you preview your text.

To underscore: BECOMING SELF-EMPLOYED

Place your cursor under the 'B' of 'BECOMING' and:

PRESS : START EMBEDDED COMMAND, red function key **f1**

TYPE : OC27,45,1

PRESS : END EMBEDDED COMMAND, red function key **f2**

Move your cursor to the end of the heading (the space after the 'D' of 'EMPLOYED') and then:

PRESS : START EMBEDDED COMMAND, red function key **f1**

TYPE : OC27,45,Ø

PRESS : END EMBEDDED COMMAND, red function key **f2**

```
Words-145    Characters free-23218 I



Start
LM10 LL60 JO
   OC27,45,1 BECOMING SELF
EMPLOYED OC27,45,0 _


To become self-employed is the aim of
many people and setting up in business
can change your life.

Where to start?

First of all you as the prospective
entrepreneur must decide on the type of
business you will establish and ask
```

Photo 7 shows the screen in Edit Mode with the Wordwise Embedded Commands for the underscore.

19

WORDWISE PLUS users: to underscore 'BECOMING SELF-EMPLOYED', place your cursor under the 'B' of 'BECOMING' and:

PRESS : START EMBEDDED COMMAND, red function key **f1**

TYPE : US

PRESS : END EMBEDDED COMMAND, red function key **f2**

Move your cursor to the end of the heading (the space after the 'D' of 'EMPLOYED') and:

PRESS : START EMBEDDED COMMAND, red function key **f1**

TYPE : UE

PRESS : END EMBEDDED COMMAND, red function key **f2**

NOTE: the underscore embedded command when using WORD-WISE PLUS is US (Underscore Start), and UE (Underscore End).

```
Words-145    Characters free-23236 I




    Start
    LM10 LL60 JO
      US BECOMING SELF EMPLOYED UE _

    To become self-employed is the aim of
    many people and setting up in business
    can change your life.
                                        o
    Where to start?

    First of all you as the prospective
    entrepreneur must decide on the type of
    business you will establish and ask
    yourself is there really a market for my
```

Photo 8 shows the screen in Edit Mode with the Wordwise Plus Embedded Commands for underscore.

3.4 Deleting marked text

To delete the final paragraph, place your cursor under the 'T' of 'There' and set a marker by pressing **f3** . Move your cursor to the

space at the end of the paragraph and set another marker: PRESS :
f3 .

Now PRESS : DELETE MARKED TEXT, **f7** .

Gone? Good! Now PRESS: **ESCAPE** and move into Menu Mode.
Look at the options and opt for 7) PREVIEW TEXT. Remember
if it scrolls too fast for you to see, WORDWISE users PRESS :
CTRL and **SHIFT** and scrolling will stop; WORDWISE PLUS
users PRESS: space bar to stop scrolling. Check your final version
against the one on page 82.

3.5 Saving (Option 1)

Save your work on to disk, that's option 1. (See page 15 if you
have forgotten how to do this.) Call this file S3 followed by your
initials. Make sure you have a disk in the disk drive prior to trying
to save a file.

3.6 Printing (Option 6)

To print your text you need option 6) PRINT TEXT. Make sure
that your printer has been set up and that it has paper in it. If
everything is ready

PRESS : 6

One of the good points about WORDWISE and WORDWISE PLUS
is that you do not have to save work prior to printing. If you did
not want to save the passage on to disk, you could just PRESS : 6
(PRINT TEXT) and your passage would be printed out but you
would not have a copy of it on disk.

3.7 Problems with printer

If your printer has not been set up properly you may find that
your text is being printed one line on top of another. To remedy
this, in Menu Mode, TYPE : *FX6, $\emptyset$ -- this instruction makes the
printer 'line feed' and should solve the problem.

There are many different computer printers on the market and you may find that your particular model does not print out properly. If this is the case, then consult the section on printing in your manual, or contact your dealer regarding an appropriate printer driver and dip switch settings.

An additional exercise follows if you would like further practice before starting the next section. Just type in the exercise and make any corrections or alterations using the commands learnt so far.

Additional material – exercise 3

Copy type the following passage, correct and edit using the commands learnt so far.

When you have completed this course of lessons you will have covered several of the major aspects of word processing.

It is very likely that you will go on to use different systems and whilst the commands may differ slightly, and some systems are able to perform more complex tasks than others, the word processing concepts that you have learnt will allow you to adapt your new skills.

When faced with an unfamiliar system – consult the manual first! With microcomputers, such as the BBC, a word processing package is fitted into the computer and the manual is usually small and easy to read. Most of the dedicated systems have rather large, heavy-going manuals. DON'T PANIC! Pick out from the manual the functions you are already familiar with and make yourself a prompt card with these new commands. Then go on to explore the new facilities offered by the system and make yourself another prompt card with the commands for these new functions. You will then be on your way to mastering another word processing system!

Now insert the heading **WORD PROCESSING** and underscore it.

22

3.8 Saving marked text

Finished typing? Proof read your work and then you might like to try another option from the Menu — option 3) SAVE MARKED TEXT. If you only want to save a part of the text, set the first marker at the beginning of the part you want to save and set the second marker at the end of the part you want to save and then move into Menu Mode by pressing ESCAPE . Make sure you have a disk in the disk drive.

Opt for number 3 from the Menu, SAVE MARKED TEXT. You will need to give your file a name and remember to PRESS : RETURN . Instead of saving the entire text only the marked portion will have been saved.

Section 4

TYPE : *W. and PRESS : **RETURN** . (WORDWISE users answer 'N' to the question 'OLD TEXT OR NOT?') PRESS : **ESCAPE** and you will be in Edit Mode.
Set your left hand margin, your line length and turn the justification on. (Refer back to Section 2 or Section 1 if necessary.)

4.1

Now copy type the following passage.

Many students are interested in working abroad once they have qualified. Some just pack-up and go with nothing in particular planned in the hope that they will find employment once they reach their destination. Others go to jobs abroad arranged through an agency in this country. However, there is another way of combining working abroad with working in this country and that is with the Foreign and Commonwealth Office.

The Foreign and Commonwealth Office employs secretaries and copy typists initially to work in London for at least a year prior to being posted to a British Diplomatic Mission anywhere in the world. I know of two ex-students who joined the Foreign and Commonwealth Office and after their time in London, one went to work at the British Office in India and the other went to the British High Commission in Australia.

During their stay at their postings they both took very interesting holidays. The secretary who was sent to India, went to the exotic south of the country with its palm-fringed beaches for her holiday. The secretary who went to Australia took a trip into the inland and Northern Territories for her vacation where she saw the special magical qualities of Ayers Rock, and further north — camels, water buffalo and salt water crocodiles.

So, if you are interested in working in London and also abroad, the minimum secretarial qualifications required by the Foreign and Commonwealth Office are: 30 wpm typing for copy typist posts and 100 wpm shorthand and 30 wpm typing for secretarial posts. Positions are advertised in the national press.

Finished copy typing? Proof read your work and make corrections using the commands already learnt.

4.2 Centred heading

Give the passage a centred heading. Place your cursor under the 'M' at the top of your text and create a line space by pressing **RETURN** . In the space that has been created you are going to put your centred heading. Centring requires another embedded command.

PRESS : **f1** TYPE : CE PRESS : **f2** and then type the heading: WORKING ABROAD ('code' for centring – CE). Make sure you have a clear line of space between the heading and the passage.

4.3 Indented paragraphs

You are now going to indent your paragraphs. Place your cursor at the top of your passage under the 'M' of 'Many'. You are now going to give an embedded command to indent this paragraph on printing. So would you please PRESS : START EMBEDDED COMMAND **f1** and TYPE : TI6 and then PRESS: END EMBEDDED COMMAND **f2** . You have now set an embedded command for a temporary indent of 6 spaces ('code' for Temporary Indent – TI). Now take your cursor to the start of each paragraph and carry out the same procedure, ie, PRESS: **f1** TYPE : TI6 and then PRESS : **f2** .

Move into Menu Mode (PRESS : **ESCAPE**) and either print this from the screen (ie, without saving it first) or save it on to disk and then print it out. Check your final version against the one on page 83.

An additional exercise follows if you would like further practice before starting the next section. Just type in the exercise and make any corrections or alterations using the commands learnt so far.

Additional material – exercise 4

Centre
Reading SPELLING DICTIONARIES CHECKERS

It is now possible to buy a spelling checker to run with most word processing packages. These spelling checkers are excellent for picking up typographical errors and are a great help for the poor speller!

The spelling checker program proof reads the text and then highlights misspelt words, or lists words which are not in its dictionary – allowing the word processor operator to correct them. Spelling checkers allow you to add extra words to the dictionary enabling to so that you can customise it for your own business.

If you are thinking of buying a spelling checker to run with your word processing package find out: 1) the number of words in its dictionary; 2) whether you can expand the dictionary; 3) how long does it take to run the spelling checker program – some systems are very slow!

26

Section 5

You should by now be using the commands to make alterations and corrections with confidence.

In Menu Mode, TYPE : *W. and PRESS : **RETURN** . (WORD-WISE users — in answer to the question OLD TEXT OR NOT? TYPE : N) PRESS : **ESCAPE** and move into Edit Mode.

In this passage you will be using the **TAB** key and you will be setting an embedded command to double line space this passage on printing.

5.1 Double line spacing and defining a tab

The new embedded command codes that you will be using are LS for the line spacing and DT to define the tab stop positions. You will be given the tab stop position points. You now have several embedded commands to list and there is a slightly quicker way than the **f1** , code, **f2** sequence. Instead of this usual sequence you can miss out the **f2** command key after each code as long as you press **f1** and insert another embedded command. However, you must end the list by pressing **f2** .

You might like to try this:
PRESS : **f1** , TYPE : LM1∅ PRESS: **f1** TYPE : LL65 PRESS : **f1** TYPE : DT6,23,36 PRESS : **f1** TYPE : JO PRESS : **f1** TYPE : LS2 PRESS : **f2** .

Quite a list! Just to recap, you have now set a left margin of 10, a line length of 65, tabs at 6, 23 and 36 character points across the scale, turned the justification on and have set double line spacing. (All at the press of a button!) Do make sure that you typed the figures after the DT code the way I have done ie, DT6,23,36 — no spaces after the commas.

5.2 Indenting

To indent your paragraph just press the **TAB** key (next to the Q key). An arrow will appear and although it will not show on your screen your paragraph will be indented by 6 spaces.

Near the end of the passage where you have to tabulate 'certificates, diplomas, notebook, pen, pencil, correction papers' — all you will need to do is press your **TAB** key, as follows:

PRESS : **TAB** TYPE : certificates PRESS : **TAB** TYPE : diplomas PRESS : **TAB** TYPE : notebook PRESS : **RETURN** . PRESS : **TAB** TYPE : pen PRESS : **TAB** TYPE : pencil PRESS : **TAB** TYPE : correction papers

Your typing will not appear in columns on your screen but on moving into Menu Mode and pressing 7 for the PREVIEW TEXT you will see your work in columns and your paragraphs indented.

Ready to type?

5.3 Centred heading

Start with a centred heading. PRESS : **f1** TYPE : CE PRESS : **f2** and then TYPE : GOING FOR AN INTERVIEW

PRESS : **RETURN** twice to give you a clear line of space between the heading and your passage.

GOING FOR AN INTERVIEW

Are you going for an interview? Be prepared!

Find out as much as you can about the company before going to the interview and make a note of questions that you would like to ask. Make sure you know how to get to the interview address — there is nothing worse than a candidate arriving late!

Take with you items needed for a possible shorthand and typing test. If you are feeling a little nervous about this, and the typewriter is not one you have used before, ask if you can type a 'warm-up' piece first to familiarise yourself with the machine and settle yourself down.

The night before your interview re-read your copy of your application letter and curriculum vitae. Make a list of the sort of questions you would ask if you were the interviewer and then rehearse your answers. You will find that at least some of these questions will come up the next day and your answers will be ready.

As a final check before you leave for your interview make sure you take the following: the address, the name of the person you are to see and:

certificates	diplomas	notebook
pen	pencil	correction papers

Proof read your text and make corrections. PRESS : **ESCAPE** to move into Menu Mode. Preview your text by pressing .7 and then save this on to disk, (PRESS : **1** to save). Call this lesson S5 followed by your initials and print it out, (option 6). Check your version with the one on page 84.

An additional exercise follows if you would like further practice before starting the next section. Just type in the exercise and make any corrections or alterations using the commands learnt so far.

Additional material – exercise 5

Before commencing this exercise make a note of the details you will need to input in order to make this a personal CV. (Use your underscore command to give emphasis to headings.)

CURRICULUM VITAE

NAME:
(Type in your name.)

ADDRESS:
(Type in your address.)

TELEPHONE:
(Type in your telephone number – include STD code.)

DATE OF BIRTH:
(Type in your date of birth in full, eg, 10 April 1969.)

MARITAL STATUS:
(Type in single or married.)

EDUCATION, QUALIFICATIONS AND TRAINING:
(List here schools attended from age 11, then details of Further Education and Higher Education. List qualifications gained and include exams to be taken this year. Add in details of all training which you have undertaken – whether examinable or not.)

WORK HISTORY:

(List here your career details to date, commencing with your present, or most recent, position and include your salary. If you have not worked, put in here details of any work experience you may have gained through school or college, or details of any voluntary work you may have been involved with.)

OTHER INFORMATION :

(At this point you may like to add details which may be of interest to a prospective employer, eg, mention which word processing systems or computers you have used; whether you can speak another language or hold a current driving licence. Some people like to give details of personal interests, eg, swimming – but this is up to you.)

REFEREES:

(If possible give the names and addresses of two people who if asked by an employer could give a reference on your behalf, eg, previous, or present employer, or your course tutor from school or college.)

End of first part of course

You have now completed 5 Sections. If you have time to finish the whole course then you will have covered several of the major aspects of the word processing operator.

If you have to leave now, however, having completed only 5 Sections, you will have a basic understanding of word processing.

Intermediate features

Housekeeping

WORDWISE users: You may now like to delete some of your files from your disk. This is called 'housekeeping'. Make sure you are in Menu Mode and then TYPE : *CAT and PRESS: `RETURN` . Look at the catalogue of files -- do you want to delete any? If you do, in Menu Mode TYPE : *DELETE followed by the name of the file and PRESS : `RETURN` . If you TYPE : *CAT and then PRESS: `RETURN` again you will see that your file has been deleted from the catalogue.

NOTE: WORDWISE PLUS users will have to return to BASIC in order to use these commands to delete files. (TYPE : *B . PRESS : `RETURN`)

Another important aspect of 'housekeeping' is taking back-up copies of the disks you want to keep. In business it is very important that a back-up copy is taken, then one copy can be filed safely and the other copy can be used as the **work disk**. Should a mistake be made and a file deleted from the work disk in error, another copy can be taken from the other disk.

The following is an example of how you would copy a disk if you are using a **Cumana double disk drive**. (If you are using a different disk drive you will have to consult the **disk drive manual**.)

Place the master disk in disk drive number 0 and the disk you are going to take the copy on to, in disk drive 1.

Move into BASIC (either by typing *BASIC and pressing `RETURN` or by typing *B. and pressing `RETURN` or by turning the computer off and then on again) and then TYPE : *ENABLE *BACKUP01 and PRESS: `RETURN` .

NOTE: if you wanted to send a copy of a file in disk form to someone who did not have WORDWISE or WORDWISE PLUS (but did have a BBC Micro) then you would save the file on to the disk using option 8 on the Menu: SPOOL TEXT. The file would be saved on to the disk in its formatted state.

Section 6

In this section and the following sections you are SARAH LEE working for JANE STEVENS the Personnel Officer at TOPS Mail Order Company.

The lessons will consist of instructions from Jane Stevens and then help with the layout or any new commands from me!

6.1

SARAH,

Please alter the following advertisement for me — I need it today please!

I've made some suggestions regarding layout — what do you think?

JS

← 40 SPACE TYPING LINE →

WANTED — centre

An Exceptional Word Processing Operator — u/c

with a minimum of 40 wpm typing who enjoys
working as part of a large team in an easy-going
atmosphere but when the pressure is on can really
pull the stops out and meet deadlines! — u/c

In return you will receive:

TOP SALARY
LUNCHEON VOUCHERS
4 WEEKS HOLIDAY
STAFF CONCESSIONS

} *centre each line please*

Interested? — *u|c → centred*

Apply by (insert next Friday's date please), enclosing

CV and the name of 2 referees, to:

Ms Jane Stevens
Personnel Officer
Tops Mail Order Company
London WC1 2XJ

} *u|c and centre each line please*

Think about this: which commands would give the best effect?
   Look at my suggestion — notice that I have added a new embedded command, well really I have modified the centring command by adding a number ie, telling the system how many lines I
want centred.

6.2

This is my suggestion:

f1 LL4Ø **f2**

f1 CE **f2**   WANTED

AN EXCEPTIONAL WORD PROCESSING OPERATOR

f1 JO **f2**

with a minimum of 40 wpm typing who enjoys
working as part of a large team in an easy-going
atmosphere BUT when the pressure is on can really
pull the stops out and MEET DEADLINES!

In return you will receive:

[f1] CE4 [f2] TOP SALARY
LUNCHEON VOUCHERS
4 WEEKS HOLIDAY
STAFF CONCESSIONS

[f1] CE [f2] INTERESTED?

Apply by (next Friday's date inserted), enclosing CV

and the names of 2 referees, to:

[f1] CE4 [f2] MS JANE STEVENS

PERSONNEL OFFICER

TOPS MAIL ORDER COMPANY

LONDON WC1 2XJ

6.3 Underscoring and emboldening type

To give emphasis to certain words you could underscore or **embolden** the type.

For example, to embolden: **AN EXCEPTIONAL WORD PROCESSING OPERATOR** — WORDWISE users would:

Place cursor under the 'A' of 'AN' and:
PRESS : [f1]
TYPE : OC27,69
PRESS : [f2]
Move cursor to the space after the 'R' of 'OPERATOR' and:
PRESS : [f1]
TYPE : OC27,7∅
PRESS : [f2]

Again this WORDWISE command is a command to the printer and will not show on previewing your text.

WORDWISE PLUS users would:

Place cursor under the 'A' of 'AN' and:

PRESS : **f1**

TYPE : **DS**

PRESS : **f2**

Move cursor to the space after the 'R' of 'OPERATOR' and:

PRESS : **f1**

TYPE : **DE**

PRESS : **f2** (DS code means Double Strike Start and DE code means Double Strike End)

You learnt to underscore in Section 3 so if you would like to underscore any of the words in the advertisement to emphasise them, just to recap:

WORDWISE underscore is **f1** OC27,45,1 **f2** . Type in the word or words to be underscored, followed by **f1** OC27,45,0 **f2** .

WORDWISE PLUS underscore sequence is **f1** US **f2** then type in the word, or words, to be underscored and then **f1** UE **f2** .

Be careful when trying to underscore a centred heading — the commands don't mix very well! You can end up with an underscore line extending from the right hand margin. WORDWISE PLUS users can try and overcome this by using the following sequence: **f1** CE **f2** **f1** US **f2** (text to be centred) **f1** UE **f2** .

When you have typed up the advertisement, move into Menu Mode and preview your display by pressing 7. Compare your final version with the one on page 85. If you are happy with it, then save the advertisement on to disk. (I would suggest calling this S6 followed by your initials) and then print out a copy.

An additional exercise follows if you would like further practice before starting the next section. Just type in the exercise and make any corrections or alterations using the commands learnt.

Additional material – exercise 6

Display attractively the following menu. Use the COPY MARKED TEXT, key **f9** , to copy the decorative lines: place a marker at the beginning and the end of the work you want to copy. Then place your cursor on the line you want the copy to appear at, and PRESS: **f9** . You will need to delete the markers after you have carried out this procedure. Just PRESS : **CTRL** and **A** to delete them.

★★★★★★★★★★○○○○○○○○○○★★★★★★★★★★

TOPS MAIL ORDER COMPANY

DIRECTORS' DINING ROOM

TODAY'S SET-LUNCH MENU

ICED MELON
ONION SOUP
CHOICE OF FRUIT JUICES

★★★★★★★★★★○○○○○○○○○○★★★★★★★★★★

SOLE NORMANDE
CHICKEN WITH TARRAGON
RATATOUILLE

★★★★★★★★★★○○○○○○○○○○★★★★★★★★★★

CHOCOLATE GATEAU
APPLE FLAN

SELECTION FROM CHEESE BOARD

★★★★★★★★★★○○○○○○○○○○★★★★★★★★★★

COFFEE

★★★★★★★★★★○○○○○○○○○○★★★★★★★★★★

Section 7

In this section you have to use a memo form. So before carrying out Jane's instructions, prepare a file with a 'skeleton' memo form on it.

7.1 'Skeleton' memo form

My suggestion which follows is for a fully-blocked memo form. PRESS : **f1** TYPE : **LM1Ø** PRESS : **f1** . TYPE : **LL6Ø** PRESS : **f2** PRESS : **RETURN** and then type up the following Memo form.

MEMORANDUM

FROM:

TO:

DATE:

REF:

SUBJECT:

. . . .

7.2 Saving a form

Having typed up this form, save it on to disk so that you can use it for any memos you send out.

Make sure you have a disk in your disk drive before trying to save your memo form.

Move into Menu Mode, PRESS : 1) SAVE ENTIRE TEXT, call the file MEMO and PRESS : **RETURN** .

7.3 Recalling a form

Now load the memo form into the memory by opting for number 2 on the list, LOAD NEW TEXT. The system will ask you for the filename. TYPE : MEMO and then PRESS : RETURN .
  Move back into Edit Mode.
  Remember when infilling forms, use your cursor control keys to move to a new line — NOT the RETURN key as the 'returns' have already been recorded on the blank form. You might like to type in a space after the colon.

7.4 Infilling a memo

Now complete the memo form with the details that Jane Stevens has given below. Save the completed memo on to disk, call it S7 followed by your initials and do a print out for Jane. Compare it with the one on page 86.

SARAH

Herewith the draft of a memo to
HELEN JOLLY the W.P. SUPERVISOR. Subject:
INTERVIEWS FOR W.P. POSITION
                                    J.S

To confirm our conversation of (insert yesterday's date) concerning the 3 shortlisted applicants for the word processing position. The interviews will take place on Friday (insert the date for Friday of next week).// The candidates are:
Ms JOANNA HARRIS, Mr JOHN PERKS and
W.P. Ms SALLY HOLMES.// I think that it is important that they meet the staff in the unit and see our system

40

prior to interview. I suggest that the candidates come along to Reception at 10 am, where Sarah will meet them and bring them over to you. The first interview will then commence at

N.P 10.30 am. //

Could you please confirm that this is in order, Helen.

An additional exercise follows if you would like further practice before starting the next section. Just type in the exercise and make any corrections or alterations using the commands learnt so far.

Additional material – exercise 7

Load your skeleton memo form into the memory and then type in the following memo:

The memo is from Jane Stevens, Personnel Officer and it is to Helen Jolly, WP Supervisor. Date the memo for today and the subject heading is: INSERVICE TRAINING.

The main body of the memo reads:

Would you please send me a copy of your Inservice Training Programme for new WP Operators, as I don't seem to have one on file.

Sally Holmes will start on (insert date here) and her first week will be an inservice training week. In addition to her time with you I will also arrange for her to tour the various sections, buildings and departments.

(Suggested editing: place markers and swap paragraphs round.)

Letters

The next 3 sections concern business letters. If you do not know the layout for a business letter please read the following before commencing the lessons.

Business letters

Today most businesses use the fully-blocked style of letter layout. This means that the reference, date, addressee, salutation, each new paragraph of the letter and the complimentary close, all commence at the left hand margin (no indenting at all).

In addition most firms have now also adopted the open punctuation style. This means that punctuation is omitted from the date, name and address of the addressee, salutation and complimentary close. The main body of the letter is punctuated in the normal way.

A suggested layout for a business letter is:

Our Ref: (PRESS : `RETURN` twice)

24 April 19. . (PRESS : `RETURN` twice)

Name of addressee
Address
Address
Address (PRESS : `RETURN` twice)

Dear Madam (PRESS : `RETURN` twice)

The main body of the letter is then typed in. PRESS : `RETURN` twice between paragraphs and twice before the complimentary close.

Yours faithfully (PRESS : `RETURN` five times — to allow a space for the signature)

J WAINWRIGHT
SALES MANAGER

A business letter would be printed on headed stationery.

Personal business letters

You may, however, send out a personal business letter (perhaps to your solicitor or bank) in which case you must include your own address and telephone number — however, still retain the fully blocked style as follows:

14 Wood Row
Handsend
BIRMINGHAM
B6 5GG   (PRESS : **RETURN** twice)

Tel: 021–123–4566   (PRESS : **RETURN** twice)

24 April 19 . .   (PRESS : **RETURN** twice)

Then insert the name and address of the addressee — as for the business letter layout.

REMEMBER: if you type a formal salutation, ie, 'Dear Madam' then you must type a formal complimentary close, ie, Yours faithfully'. However, if you address the person by name in the salutation, ie, 'Dear Ms Brown' then use 'Yours sincerely' as the complimentary close.

Advanced features

Section 8

8.1 Notes on standard paragraphs

In business a record would be kept of all the standard paragraphs saved along with details of their filename. In this way it would be possible for the person dictating the letter or document to just ask the wp operator to insert a standard paragraph (followed by the filename or code) at the point they wanted it to occur.

In this lesson WORDWISE users are going to create a standard paragraph by redefining red function key **f0** , so that it will print out a standard paragraph when pressed in conjunction with **CTRL** and **SHIFT** .

However, redefining a function key in order to create a standard paragraph is not the only way of saving paragraphs and is only really suitable for short paragraphs. If you had a longer paragraph than the one in the exercise below (or if you do not want to re-define a red function key) save the standard paragraph on to disk in the usual way (option 1 on the Menu and then give it a filename). Then when you want to insert the paragraph into your document, choose option 4 from the Menu (LOAD TEXT TO CURSOR). The standard paragraph will then be loaded into the memory at the cursor point. This is what WORDWISE PLUS users will be doing for this exercise as redefining the red function key in WORDWISE PLUS does not work in the same way as it does for WORDWISE. However, WORDWISE PLUS users will be learning a more advanced form of redefining a red function key known as **segmenting** in Section 11.

8.2 Redefining a function key

Start in Menu Mode.

In the example I am going to give you, Jane Stevens has asked you

44

to send out several letters and they all use her standard final paragraph, which is as follows:

May I take this opportunity of thanking you for your interest in TOPS Mail Order Company.

Now there is no need to keep typing out the same string of words when word processing. You are going to reprogram — or redefine — the red function key **f0** so that when you press it and also hold **CTRL** and **SHIFT** at the same time, Jane's standard paragraph will automatically appear on your screen.

To do this, make sure you are in Menu Mode and then:

TYPE: ***KEYØMay I take this opportunity of thanking you for your interest in TOPS Mail Order Company.**

PRESS : **RETURN**

You have now redefined red function key **f0** and when it is pressed in conjunction with **CTRL** and **SHIFT** the above paragraph will be printed out.

Try it! Move into Edit Mode and type up the following letter which Jane Stevens has asked you to send out. Remember you do not have to type out the final paragraph — all you do when you reach that point is put **SHIFT LOCK** on and hold **CTRL** and PRESS : red function key **f0** — all at the same time!

Ready? Set your left margin at 10, your line length at 60 and put justification on.

8.3

JS/SL

(date for today please)

Mr J Davies
93 Swan Street
Clapham
LONDON SW4 9PX

Dear Mr Davies

Thank you for your letter of (insert last Monday's date please) enquiring about a possible vacancy in the Catering Section.

Unfortunately at the present time we do not have a vacancy. However, I will keep your letter on file and should a suitable vacancy occur in the near future I will contact you again.

May I take this opportunity of thanking you for your interest in TOPS Mail Order Company.

Yours sincerely

Jane Stevens
Personnel Officer

Did you remember to use your standard paragraph key? Move into Menu Mode and save this letter on to disk and then print it out. I would suggest calling this file S8 followed by your initials. Compare your version with the one on page 87.

Additional material – exercise 8

An additional exercise follows if you would like further practice before starting the next section. Just type in the exercise and make any corrections or alterations using the commands learnt so far.

JS/SL
19 JUNE 19 --

Mrs S Swan
15 Rainbow Hill
Lewisham
London SE13 OTP

Dear Mrs Swan,

Thank you for your letter of 12 June enquiring about a possible vacancy in our

N.P. Accounts Dept. // As it happens there will be a temporary vacancy in the Accounts Division for a period of six months, commencing 1 August. If you are interested in this position I would be grateful if you would kindly complete the enclosed application form and return it to me as soon as possible

TE.
RAH   * INSERT STANDARD PARAGRAPH HERE *
Yours sincerely

Jane Stevens
Personnel Officer

Enc

47

Section 9

9.1 Creating a standard letter

In this section you are going to type up a 'skeleton' letter for use in the Personnel Office. This letter is going to be a standard letter calling candidates for interview.

Remember you will have to leave a space for the reference, the date and the addressee. I would suggest turning up 10 line spaces after the 'Our Ref', (ie, PRESS : **RETURN** 10 times). Before beginning to type the letter remember to set your left margin, line length and turn the justification on.

Our Ref:

Dear

Re:

In connection with your application for the above post would you please attend for interview on:

On arrival please follow the signs for the Reception Area where you will be met by:

I would be pleased if you would confirm whether you are able to attend as soon as possible.

Yours sincerely

Jane Stevens
Personnel Officer

9.2 Saving a standard letter

Finished typing? Move into Menu Mode and it is important to save this letter on to disk, as you are now going to send out three copies of your standard letter. So having made sure that you have a disk in your disk drive PRESS : 1 for SAVE ENTIRE TEXT and call this file S9 followed by your initials. PRESS : **RETURN** .

9.3 Recalling a standard letter

Now PRESS : 2 for LOAD NEW TEXT and load your standard letter.

9.4 'Personalising' a standard letter

The first copy of the letter is for:

Ms J Harris
2 Kings Road
EPSOM
KT19 2PT

Remember when infilling details move to a new line using the cursor control keys and *NOT* the **RETURN** key. To 'person-alise' your standard letter for Ms Harris, move your cursor to the space after 'Our Ref:' and TYPE : JS/SL. Move your cursor down two lines and then insert today's date. Move your cursor down another two lines and type in Ms Harris's name and address. Move your cursor down two more lines and after 'Dear' insert **Ms Harris** .

9.5 Cursor to ? key

After you have typed Ms Harris on the salutation line, PRESS : red function key **f4** , the CURSOR TO? key. On the status line you will see the question CURSOR TO?

TYPE : :   and your cursor will automatically move to the next occurrence of : which is after Re: on the subject heading line.

Move your cursor to the space after this and:

TYPE : **WORD PROCESSING VACANCY**

PRESS : CURSOR TO? key **f4** again and then:

TYPE: : and your cursor will move to the next occurrence of : which is after the word 'on' and now you can insert the date and time of the interview. Use next Friday's date (please insert the appropriate date) and the time will be 10 am.

Now PRESS : CURSOR TO? key **f4** again, and then:

TYPE : : This time your cursor will move to the next occurrence of : which is after the word 'by' and here please TYPE : the name Ms Lee . (You might like to delete the : before inserting 'Ms Lee'.)

Your letter should now be a totally 'personalised' standard letter ready to be sent to Ms Harris. Move into Menu Mode and print this letter out either saving it first on to disk or printing directly from screen. Check your version with the one on page 88.

You now have another 2 candidates to call for interview. Use the same procedure as for the letter you sent out to Ms Harris.

The candidates are:

Mr J Perks
12 Carlton Way
MAIDENHEAD
SL5 2PX

Ms S Holmes
6 Fairway
Acton
LONDON W3 5GY

Remember to call up your standard letter first by opting for number 2 on the Menu (LOAD NEW TEXT) and then type S9 followed by your initials.

Save the letters for Ms Holmes and Mr Perks on to disk and then print out all three letters.

An additional exercise follows if you would like further practice before starting the next section. Just type in the exercise and make any corrections or alterations using the commands learnt so far.

Additional material – exercise 9

Save a skeleton of this letter on to disk, load it into the memory and then 'personalise' it to each of the unsuccessful candidates. If you worked through Section 8 you might like to use your standard paragraph for the last paragraph of the letter.

The letter is as follows:

Our Ref:

Dear

Re:

Thank you for attending for interview concerning the above post.

After careful consideration, however, I regret to inform you that you were unsuccessful on this occasion.

May I take this opportunity of thanking you for your interest in TOPS Mail Order Company.

Yours sincerely

Jane Stevens
Personnel Officer

The unsuccessful candidates are

Ms J Harris	Mr J Perks
2 Kings Road	12 Carlton Way
EPSOM	MAIDENHEAD
KT19 2PT	SL5 9PX

Section 10

Move into Edit Mode and type up this draft letter which Jane
Stevens has asked you to do. Set an appropriate left hand margin,
line length and turn the justification on. When you have typed it,
save it on to disk as S10 followed by your initials and then load it
back into the memory ready for revision.

10.1 Draft letter for you to type up

JS/SL
date for today

Ms Sally Holmes
6 Fairway
Acton
London W3 5QY

Dear Ms Holmes

In full RE: (WP) POST

Further to your interview on (insert date) I
am pleased to inform you that you have
N.P. been selected for the above post. // The
interviewing panel were most impressed
with you and really felt that you
in full would fit in well with our (WP) team.
I am attaching two copies of
your employment contract giving full

details of salary, holiday entitlement etc.// If you wish to accept this post would you please sign both copies of the contract, retain one for yourself and return the other one to me as soon as possible.// We look forward to you commencing with us in four weeks' time on Monday (date).

In the meantime, if you have any queries regarding this post please do not hesitate to contact me.

Yours sincerely

JS

10.2 Letter for revision

Please read the instructions in 10.3 – 10.5 before beginning to alter your text.

JS/SL

(date)

Ms Sally Holmes
6 Fairway
Acton
LONDON W3 5GY

Dear Ms Holmes
RE: WORD PROCESSING ~~POST~~ POSITION

Further to your interview on (date of interview inserted) I am

pleased to inform you that you have been selected for the above
~~post.~~ *position*

The interviewing panel were most impressed with you and really felt that you would fit in well with our word processing team.   *delete*

I am attaching two copies of your employment contract giving
full details of salary, holiday entitlement, etc. *health insurance*
N.P. *scheme, superannuation plan and staff concessions on Tops mail order goods.* //

position
If you wish to accept this ~~post~~ would you please sign both copies
of the contract, retain one for yourself and return the other one
to me as soon as possible.

We look forward to you commencing with us in four weeks' time
on Monday (appropriate date inserted).

run on   *position*
In the meantime, if you have any queries regarding this ~~post~~ please
do not hesitate to contact me.

Yours sincerely

Jane Stevens
Personnel Officer
Enc

We are arranging an in service word processing familiarisation programme so that you may adapt your skills to our system. This will take place during your first week with us.

54

10.3 Search and replace (Option 5)

In editing this letter you have an opportunity to use a very useful command to search through the text and change one word for another word. In the revised letter you have been asked to change 'post' to 'position' each time it occurs. To do this, make sure that your cursor is at the top of your letter in Edit Mode, then move into Menu Mode and look at the options.

Option 5 on the Menu list SEARCH AND REPLACE is the option which you want to use. Make sure the cursor is at the top of the text. PRESS : 5 and the question GLOBAL OR SELECTIVE (G/S) will be asked, in other words all occurrences of the word or just some. You want to change every occurrence of 'post' to 'position' so PRESS : G. You will then be asked to PLEASE ENTER SEARCH STRING and you should then TYPE : post and PRESS : **RETURN** . Then PLEASE ENTER REPLACE STRING is displayed. TYPE : position and PRESS : **RETURN** . This will change

```
              WORDWISE-PLUS
        (C) Computer Concepts 1984


      1)  Save entire text
      2)  Load new text
      3)  Save marked text
      4)  Load text to cursor
      5)  Search and Replace
      6)  Print text
      7)  Preview text
      8)  Spool text
    ` 9)  Segment menu

      ESC Edit Mode
      Global or selective? (G/S)G

      Please enter search string
      post


      Please enter replace string
      position_
```

Photo 9 shows the screen in Menu Mode having chosen Option 5: SEARCH AND REPLACE.

all occurrences of post to position automatically. But it probably will not have changed the word when it occurred in upper case. To do this you will need to move back into Menu Mode and PRESS: 5 again, opt for G and then TYPE : **POST** and PRESS : **RETURN** TYPE : **POSITION** and PRESS: **RETURN** .

10.4 Deleting marked text

Now make the other revisions asked for. Delete paragraph 2 by setting a marker at the beginning and end of the passage and PRESS : **f7** .

10.5 Merging paragraphs

To join the paragraph commencing 'In the meantime . . .' on to the previous paragraph place the cursor at the end of the sentence on the penultimate paragraph and PRESS : **CTRL** and **A** . The last paragraph will move up a line and if it has not quite linked up to the other paragraph, PRESS : **CTRL** and **A** again.

When you have completed revising the letter, save it on to disk as S10 followed by your initials and print it out.

Compare your finished letter with the one on page 89.
An additional exercise follows if you would like further practice.

Additional material – exercise 10

(centre heading)

WORD PROCESSING 2 ——>

(double line spacing)

Having learnt to use your word processor, you will make the best use of it by using it for REPETITIVE TYPING, REVISION TYPING and ORIGINAL TYPING.

REPETITIVE TYPING
Repetitive Typing

~~This~~ includes standard paragraphs, standard letters and standard reports that are used over and over again. These standard documents are ~~then~~ saved on to disk and loaded into the memory as and when required.

REVISION TYPING

Revision Typing includes all letters, reports and other business documents *which* ~~that~~ have more than one draft – the text being revised by deleting, inserting or moving paragraphs. ~~possibly totally deleting a paragraph~~.

ORIGINAL TYPING

Original Typing includes general business correspondence which is ~~usually~~ only typed once. However, as the final letter, or document, will be error-free and have a justified right hand margin, a more professional finish will be given to your typing.

These are some of the reasons why using a word processor will prove invaluable to the professional production of your correspondence, reports and business documents.

Section 11

Wordwise Plus segment menu

In Menu Mode you have 9 options, the first 8 are the same as WORDWISE — and we have already dealt with these — but the ninth option offered by WORDWISE PLUS is the Segment Menu. This is the option which marks the real difference between WORDWISE and WORDWISE PLUS. Segments in this mode used in conjunction with the Wordwise Plus Program Disk offer such facilities as Mail Merge and Alphabetical Sorting.

NOTE: the Wordwise Plus Program Disk should be in the box that the Wordwise Plus ROM and manual came in. If you have a Wordwise Plus Program Cassette and not a disk program, transfer it on to disk or contact Computer Concepts (makers of WORDWISE PLUS) and ask if you can exchange the cassette program for a disk program.

Now to move into Segment Menu:

PRESS : 9 and you will move into the Segment Menu and another 9 options will appear on your screen.

```
              SEGMENT MENU
        (C) Computer Concepts 1984

        1)   Save segment
        2)   Load segment
        3)   Save marked text
        4)   Load text to cursor
        5)   Select segment   (0)
        6)   Print segment
        7)   Preview segment
        8)   Delete segment
        9)   Main menu

        ESC Edit Mode

        Please enter choice_
```

Photo 10 shows the screen in Wordwise Plus Segment Menu.

11.1 What is segmenting?

By dividing (or segmenting) the memory up into 10 segments, from 0 – 9, which relate to the red function keys 0 – 9 you can now save either text or instructions as segments.

11.2 Segment menu options

Options 1 – 4 and options 6 and 7 on the Segment Menu offer the same functions as their corresponding options on the Main Menu *EXCEPT* they save or load text using the segments.
 Option 5 tells you which segment you are using.
 Option 8 deletes a segment.
 Option 9 will return you to the Main Menu.

11.3 Mail merge

We are now going to look at the special feature of WORDWISE PLUS which provides the very useful Mail Merge facility.
 Mail Merge is perhaps the most useful function of a word processor. What it means is that a standard letter file can be automatically merged with a name and address file and then personalised letters can be printed out for each person on the address list.
 The two files you will need are an address list file and the file with the letter to be merged.
 In business you would probably have your clients' addresses on disk but for this exercise I will ask you to type in and save a short address list and then type in the letter to be merged with the address list.

11.4 Address list file

Make sure you are in Main Menu (NOT Segment Menu). Now PRESS : ESCAPE and move into Edit Mode. Type in the following address list.

NOTE: the name and address *MUST* take up exactly 4 lines for each person and there *MUST* be one clear line of space between each address.

Ready?

Set left margin at 10, ie, **f1** LM1Ø **f2** . Now type in the following:

Mrs B Bickford
37 Westhill Close
GUILDFORD
Surrey GU1 2AP

Ms C Canon
2 Tile Hurst
AXFORD
Notts AX9 5PX

Dr P Duncton
22 Brighton Avenue
CHESTER
CH15 8ER

Miss C Elsworth
24 Meadow Way
WOKING
Berks WK14 5AB

Mrs D Gould
4 Arcade Parade
BRACKNELL
Berks BK7 7HP

Mrs J Mancini
26 Prospect Row
HEMEL HEMPSTEAD
Herts HR2 7FT

Ms A O'Toole
137 Brook Green

WEYMOUTH
Dorset WE5 3BQ

Mrs J Renwick
6 Ferndale Road
WOLVERHAMPTON
WL7 9MP

Mrs A Spooner
1 Compton Close
REDRUTH
Cornwall TR14 1XY

Miss J Walker
10 Oakley Way
Moseley
BIRMINGHAM B13 1HY

Move back into Menu Mode and save this address list on to disk.
Call this file ADDRESS.

With the address list safely filed on to disk, clear the memory
and then type in the letter file.

11.5 Letter file

In Edit Mode type in this standard letter which you are going to
send out to the clients on your address list file.

Set your left margin at 10, the line length at 60 and turn the
justification on, ie **f1** LM10 **f1** LM60 **f1** JO **f2**

Ready?

(Type in the date)

Dear Madam

Further to your recent application I am pleased to inform you
that you have been selected as a Mail Order Agent for TOPS Mail
Order Company.

We look forward to receiving your first order and take this opportunity to remind you that you will receive 10% commission on all goods sold by you. Don't forget, as soon as we receive your first order we will despatch your FREE gift of a coffee percolator as requested.

Please return your first order to me in the enclosed pre-paid envelope as soon as possible.

Yours faithfully

Hilary Somers
Sales Manager

Enc

Now PRESS : **RETURN** 34 times. (This is because this letter will fit on continuous stationery which is 9.5 inches x 11 inches (241 mm x 279 mm) and has 66 lines on it.) If you do not turn up these extra line spaces at the end of the letter the letters in your mail merge will be printed directly underneath each other — and not on separate sheets of paper.
NOTE: if you are using a different size paper then you will have to modify the number of line spaces you turn up according to the length of your paper.

Now move into Menu Mode and save this letter on to disk. Call this file SALES1

11.6 Merging letter file and address file

To merge the letter with your address list so that you have 10 personalised letters, carry out the following steps:

1   Check that you have saved your address list on to disk.
2   Check that you have saved your letter on to disk.
3   Remove your disk from the disk drive.
4   Insert the Wordwise Plus Program Disk into your disk drive.
5   In Menu Mode, PRESS : 9 for Segment Menu.
6   In Segment Menu, select 5 from the Segment Menu list (ie, SELECT SEGMENT)

7   PRESS : Ø (ie, you have now selected Segment Number Ø).
    NOTE: always commence loading segments with Segment
    Number Ø.
8   Select number 2 from the Menu (ie, select LOAD SEGMENT).
9   When you are asked the filename:

TYPE : **MAIL1**

PRESS : **RETURN**

OK. What have you done so far?

You have selected the program MAIL1 from the Wordwise Plus
Program Disk and you have now loaded this into Segment Number
   This is the program which will instruct the computer to merge
your address file and the letter file.

10   Remove the Wordwise Plus Program Disk from your disk
     drive (the program, MAIL1, remember, has now been saved
     in Segment Ø).
11   Insert your disk into the disk drive.
12   Look at the Segment Menu and select number 5 (ie, SELECT
     SEGMENT).
13   The segment you want to select is number 9, so now   PRESS:
     9 . In this segment you are going to save the address list.
     NOTE: the program for Mail Merge (ie, MAIL1) is such that
     the computer always looks in Segment Number 9 for the
     address list — so you must *ALWAYS* put the address list in
     Segment Number 9: to do this carry out Step 14 below.
14   From the Segment Menu, select option number 2 (ie, LOAD
     SEGMENT).
15   When you are asked the filename,

TYPE : **ADDRESS** (ie, the filename for the Address List)

PRESS : **RETURN**

OK. What have you done so far?

In Segment Number Ø you have the program MAIL1 and in
Segment Number 9 you have the address list. Now you need
the letter which will be in Edit Mode.

16   Return to the Main Menu from Segment Menu, ie,   PRESS: 9 .
17   If your letter is not in the memory (PRESS : **ESCAPE** to
     see if it is there) then you will need to load it. To load it,

make sure you are in Menu Mode, and then:

PRESS : 2 (ie, LOAD FILE)

TYPE : SALES1 (ie, the name of your letter file)

PRESS : RETURN

18 Move into Edit Mode (PRESS : ESCAPE). Make sure your cursor is at the top of your text.

19 PRESS : SHIFT and red function key f0 *AT THE SAME TIME.* On screen you will see the program for MAIL1 displayed. Move your cursor to line 3 (ie, the line showing: A%=OPENIN"ADRDATA"). Found it? Now overwrite the word "ADRDATA" with the name of *YOUR* file, ie, "ADDRESS". Now move your cursor to the top of your text. As soon as you carry out Step 20, the printer will commence printing the first letter – so make sure you have paper in your printer *BEFORE* commencing the next step.

```
Words-49      Characters free-22856 O


SEG O
REM "MAIL1" Mail Merge 1

CLOSE#O
A%=OPENIN"ADDRESS"
SELECT TEXT
DELETE MARKERS
CURSOR TOP
FKEY 3
FKEY 3
REPEAT
    FKEY 7
    CURSOR TOP
```

Photo 11 shows the screen after "ADRDATA" has been replaced by: "ADDRESS"

20 PRESS : SHIFT and red function key f0 *AT THE SAME TIME.* Your first Mail Merge!

11.7 Mail merge points to remember

The mail merge program (MAIL1) is on the Wordwise Plus Program Disk and must be saved into a segment – if all of the segments are empty then you must start with Segment Number 0.

When typing in an address list — a name and address can consist of 2 or more lines but *EVERY* address *MUST* consist of the same number of lines, eg, in my example the addresses are all of 4 lines. The addresses must have one clear line of space between them (ie, PRESS : **RETURN** twice).

Your address list must *ALWAYS* be loaded into Segment Number 9.

When typing in your letter you must work out how much space your letter will take up on the paper — previewing will show you exactly how the letter will appear on the paper, just remember to add in the lines of the address when counting up lines and spaces.

On pressing **SHIFT** plus the appropriate red function key, remember to alter line 3 "ADRDATA" to the name of *YOUR* file.

11.8 Alphabetical sorting

WORDWISE PLUS also offers the facility to rearrange items for you in alphabetical order.

We will presume that you have a list of clothes manufacturers that TOPS Mail Order Company deals with and you would like to save them on to disk in alphabetical order. There is no need to rearrange them prior to inputting the list — WORDWISE PLUS will do it for you!

Ready?

From Menu Mode (*NOT* Segment Mode) move into Edit Mode. *NOTE*: When using the program to alphabetically rearrange a list, it is important that you do *NOT* set a margin or put in any embedded commands. If you do the system will try to alphabetically rearrange the embedded commands as well as your list — and the program will not turn out as planned!

Please type in the following:

MINERVA FASHIONS
48 Bishops Court
BRADFORD
BD7 5RU

LOOKS
42 Bishops Court
BRADFORD
BD7 5RU

AGENTS A
19 Sun Street
LONDON
W1P 4TT

RAE
49 Eastcastle Street
LONDON
W1B 1PF

BLUJEANS
45 Castle Square
BRADFORD
BD5 8WX

YOOTH
Great Portland Street
LONDON
W1R 9PX

JUMPING JACKS
The Fashion House
5 Four Lanes
MANCHESTER MA10 9YY

PARROT DESIGNS
Parrot House
Eastcastle Street
LONDON W1B 1PP

FLAMINGO
26 Four Lanes
MANCHESTER
MA10 9YT

FIRE FASHION
Old Fire Station
MANCHESTER
MA10 8ZP

Move back into Menu Mode and save this address list on to your disk – call it FASHION.

With the FASHION file safely saved on to disk – it is time to rearrange it in to alphabetical order.

11.9 Alphabetical rearrangement of list

1 Check that you have saved the address list on to disk.
2 Remove your disk from the disk drive.
3 Insert the Wordwise Plus Program Disk into the disk drive.
4 From Menu Mode, PRESS : 9 and move into the Segment Menu.
5 Select number 5 from the Segment Menu (ie, SELECT SEGMENT).
6 Now before selecting a segment – are all your segments clear? If you are carrying out this exercise directly after the Mail Merge exercise then Segments 0 and 9 will be full – so, you will select Segment Number 1 (just PRESS : 1). If, however, you do not have anything saved in the segments as yet, then you must commence with the first segment, which is Segment Number 0 (just PRESS : 0). I will presume that you are using Segment Number 1.
7 From the Segment Menu, now select option 2 (ie, LOAD SEGMENT).
8 When you are asked the filename,
TYPE : **ADRSORT**
PRESS : RETURN

This is the name of the Wordwise Plus program which will sort your list into alphabetical order.

9   Remove the Wordwise Plus Program Disk from your disk drive (remember, you have now saved the ADRSORT program into Segment 1 — or Segment 0).

10   Insert your disk into the disk drive.

11   Return to the Main Menu from Segment Menu, ie, PRESS : 9.

12   If your Fashion House Address List is not in the memory (PRESS : **ESCAPE** to see if it is there) then you will need to load it. Make sure you are in Menu Mode, and then:
PRESS : 2 (ie, LOAD FILE)
TYPE : **FASHION**
PRESS : **RETURN**

13   Move into Edit Mode (PRESS : **ESCAPE**). Make sure your cursor is at the top of your screen.

14   You are now ready to alphabetically rearrange the list:
PRESS : **SHIFT** and red function key **f1** (ie, the segment that ADRSORT is saved under).

15   The word "SORTING" will automatically appear on your screen, followed by the first line of each address as the program rearranges the list. When the list has been rearranged in alphabetical order, your screen will return to Menu Mode.
PRESS : **ESCAPE** to see the completed rearrangement.

16   Now you can save this rearranged list over the top of your previous file FASHION.

11.10 Additional material – exercise 11

If you would like further practice with Mail Merge try the following exercise (referring back to the Mail Merge exercise for guidance where necessary). Merge your new alphabetical Fashion House Address List with the following letter:

(Date the letter for today)

Dear Sir or Madam

The Directors of TOPS Mail Order Company would like to arrange a meeting with all the Fashion Houses involved with supplying clothes and accessories for next season's catalogue.

The suggested date is Friday, 19 May at our Marylebone Road offices in London. The meeting would commence at 10.30 am and the main topic would be 'The Changing Mail Order Market Place'.

If you are interested in attending and would like the conference details sent to you as soon as they are available, please complete the enclosed reply-paid card.

Yours faithfully

Jenny Hodgson
Marketing

Enc

Section 12

12.1 Differences between Wordwise Plus and Wordwise

For users who are thinking of trading-in their WORDWISE system for a WORDWISE PLUS system, these are some of the useful features offered by WORDWISE PLUS:

1   Mail Merge and Alphabetical Sorting facilities offered by using the Segment Menu (see Section 11).

2   In Edit Mode, pressing **CTRL** and **R** deletes any markers.

3   In Edit Mode, pressing **CTRL** and **W** obtains a word re-count.

4   If you already have text in the memory and try to load another file over the top of it (option 2 from Menu Mode) you will be reminded that you already have a file in the memory, thus saving you from wiping it out with the new file (as happens with WORDWISE).

5   Likewise if you try to save a file (option 1 in Menu Mode) over the top of another, ie, by using the same file name, the system will remind you that you already have a file saved under that name.

6   You can set up to 14 Tab characters in one piece; with WORDWISE you can only set up to 9.

7   Pressing the space bar on previewing (option 7 from Main Menu) stops scrolling; with WORDWISE you have to PRESS : **CTRL** and **SHIFT** together.

8   New embedded commands with WORDWISE PLUS include:

    To embolden type (or double-strike)

    PRESS : **f1**
    TYPE : DS
    PRESS : **f2**
    TYPE : (words to be emboldened)

PRESS : **f1**
TYPE : DE
PRESS : **f2**

To underscore:
PRESS : **f1**
TYPE : US
PRESS : **f2**
TYPE : (words to be underscored)
PRESS : **f1**
TYPE : UE
PRESS : **f2**

9   To clear text from the memory once you no longer want it, and in order to type in new text, unlike WORDWISE where you just PRESS: **BREAK** or, in Menu Mode: TYPE : *W. and PRESS : **RETURN** and the text is automatically cleared, with WORDWISE PLUS you have to actually tell the system to delete the text as follows:

In Edit Mode place your cursor at the end of the passage (**SHIFT** and **↓** together).

TYPE : **#** (or another similarly obscure character which is not actually part of your text!).

Move your cursor to the top of your passage (**SHIFT** and **↑** together).

PRESS : red function key **f6** DELETE TO? key.

TYPE : **#** — and your text is cleared.

12.2 Help index

TEXT MODE

CTRL plus **A** — deletes a character.
CTRL plus **D** — deletes a word.
CTRL plus **S** — changes case.
Red function keys will not work if the **SHIFT LOCK** is on.
They will work, however, with **CAPS LOCK** on.
Red function key **f0** — press to change from Insert Mode to
Over Mode. In Over Mode you can 'overtype'. Return to Insert
Mode by pressing **f0** again.
Red function key **f1** — press to start an embedded command,
then type in the command code.
Red function key **f2** — press to end an embedded command.

Embedded command codes

NOTE: the commands to underscore and to embolden type are
commands directed at the printer and relate to an Epson dot
matrix printer. If you have a different printer, consult your
printer manual.

WORDWISE users

UNDERSCORE — place your cursor under the first letter of
the word/s you want to underscore and PRESS : **f1** TYPE :
OC27,45,1 and then PRESS : **f2** . Move cursor to the end of
the word/s you want to underscore and PRESS : **f1** TYPE :
OC27,45,Ø and PRESS : **f2** .
EMBOLDEN — place your cursor under the first letter of the
word/s you want to embolden and PRESS : **f1** . TYPE : OC27,69
and PRESS : **f2** . Move your cursor to the end of the word/s
you want emboldened and then PRESS : **f1** and TYPE :
OC27,7Ø and PRESS : **f2** .

WORDWISE PLUS users

UNDERSCORE — PRESS : **f1** TYPE : US PRESS : **f2** TYPE :
(words to be underscored) then PRESS : **f1** TYPE : UE
PRESS : **f2** .
EMBOLDEN — PRESS : **f1** TYPE : DS PRESS : **f2** TYPE :

(words to be emboldened)   then PRESS : **f1** TYPE :   DE
PRESS : **f2** .

CE — Centre — followed by word/s you want centred. Alternatively, CE followed by a number indicates that you want the following x-number of lines centred.

JO — Justification On. NJ — No justification.

LL — Line Length — followed by the number you want the line length to be set at, eg, 60.

LM — Left Margin — followed by the number of spaces you want the left margin set at, eg, 10.

LS — Line Spacing — followed by the number you want the line spacing to be at, eg, LS2 would be double-line spacing, LS3 would be triple line spacing, etc.

SS — Single Spacing — in order to return to single line spacing when you have been working in double-line spacing.

TI — Temporary Indent — followed by the number of spaces you want the indent to be, eg, TI6 would indent the paragraph by 6 spaces.

For details of further embedded commands, read the section on embedded commands in the Wordwise Manual.

RED FUNCTION KEY **f3** — sets marker, used in conjunction with **f7** or **f8** or **f9** ie, DELETE MARKED TEXT, MOVE MARKED TEXT or COPY MARKED TEXT. Set a marker at the beginning of the text and then one at the end. Then move your cursor to the place you want the text moved to or copied to and press the appropriate key. (You will have to use the **DELETE** key to delete markers after the copy manoeuvre.)

RED FUNCTION KEY **f4** — produces CURSOR TO? on the status line. Type in the character you want the cursor to move to and — it moves there automatically.

RED FUNCTION KEY **f5** — produces WORD COUNT TO? on the status line. Insert the character you want the word count to — and the new word count appears on the status line.

RED FUNCTION KEY **f6** — produces DELETE TO? on the status line. Insert the character you want the text deleted up to —

and everything from the cursor up to the specified character will be deleted. (This key is useful for clearing old text from the screen.)

Menu mode

OPTION 1 — saves entire text on to disk. Make sure you have a disk in the disk drive first. You will be asked to give the file a name of no more than 7 characters and then PRESS : **RETURN** .
OPTION 2 — loads text previously saved on to disk into the memory. You will be asked for the name of the file you want loaded, then PRESS : **RETURN** .

OPTION 3 — saves a marked part of the text only. PRESS : 3 , give the filename and then PRESS : **RETURN** .

OPTION 4 — the LOAD TO CURSOR option. PRESS : 4 , give name of file you want loaded, PRESS : **RETURN** and the text from the disk is added on to the existing text in the memory. The new text is loaded into the memory at the point where the cursor is.

OPTION 5 — the SEARCH AND REPLACE option. *NOTE*: before choosing this option you must make sure that the cursor is at the top of your text in Edit Mode. Then move into Menu Mode and PRESS : 5 . GLOBAL OR SELECTIVE is displayed. PRESS : G for global and then type in the word/s you want the system to search for. PRESS : **RETURN** . Next type in the word/s you want to replace them with. PRESS : **RETURN** . Option G replaces all occurrences of the word/s automatically. Option S, the selective option, moves the cursor to the first occurrence of the word and by pressing **Y** the word is changed, but by pressing any other key the word is not changed.

OPTION 6 — prints text from screen ie, text does not have to be saved on to disk prior to printing.

OPTION 7 — previews your text by 'scrolling' it in its formatted state. To stop scrolling, WORDWISE users PRESS : **CTRL** and **SHIFT** together, WORDWISE PLUS users PRESS : **SPACE BAR**.

74

OPTION 8 — saves on to disk the formatted text.

OPTION 9 — (WORDWISE PLUS users) moves from Menu Mode into Segment Mode.

*CAT PRESS : **RETURN** — lists all the files on disk. (Make sure you have the disk in the disk drive first!)

*DELETE followed by the filename and then PRESS: **RETURN** — deletes that file from the disk. WORDWISE PLUS users will have to return to BASIC in order to use this command.

*W. PRESS: **RETURN** (and WORDWISE users then answering 'N' to the question OLD TEXT OR NOT?) — clears old text from the memory.

ESCAPE — pressing **ESCAPE** moves you between Menu Mode and Edit Mode.

WORDWISE PLUS users to clear text from Edit Mode:

In Edit Mode place your cursor at the end of the passage (PRESS : **SHIFT** and ▓ at the same time.)

TYPE : **#** (or another similarly obscure character which is not actually part of your text!)

Move your cursor to the top of your passage (PRESS : **SHIFT** and ▓ at the same time).

PRESS : red function key **f6** DELETE TO? key.

TYPE : **#** (or whatever obscure character you used) and your screen will be cleared.

12.3 Word processing terms

It is a good idea to familiarise yourself with some of the word processing/computing jargon that is around. However, I am pleased to say that this book is as jargon-free as possible!

1 Word processing

Basically the typing, editing, filing and printing of text by a computerised system using a magnetic storage medium! The word processor can be a **dedicated system** — a computer designed purely as a word processor, or a **general purpose computer** (like the BBC B) with a word processing package fitted.

2 Hardware

The 'machines' which make up the computer: the Central Processing Unit (**CPU**) or the brain of the computer; the **Visual Display Unit (VDU)** or the screen or monitor on which your typed text appears and on which you will find the flashing signal indicating your position on the screen, known as the **cursor**; the **keyboard** — the usual keyboard layout is used for **input**, that is inputting typing into the computer and the keyboard is also used for inputting the various commands. The **disk drive** — the unit which operates the filing mechanism saving your text on to **disks**. (Disk programs are **software**.) The **printer** is the unit which prints out the finished document known as the **hard copy**. Printers can use either **continuous stationery** or individual sheets of paper. Stationery is usually fed into the printer via a **tractor feed** system for continuous stationery or a **hopper feed** system for printers using sheets of paper. Printers are usually (a) **dot matrix**, in which the characters are formed by dots (you will probably have seen dot matrix printing). Dot matrix characters are printed out at approximately 150 characters per second (cps). (b) **daisy wheel**, in which the characters are arranged in a petal formation. Daisy wheel printers are **impact** printers and they give a high quality finish. The daisy wheel printer prints characters at approximately

50-60 cps. (c) **ink jet** — where the ink is literally sprayed on to the paper. The ink jet printer also gives a high quality print finish and prints at approximately 90-100 cps. Most printers are **bi-directional** — that is they print backwards and forwards.

3 Software

Programs held on disk (or tape) are software. **Disks** can be **floppy disks** or **hard disks**. (You will be using a **floppy disk mini-diskette** for these lessons.) The floppy disk holds the equivalent of approximately 70-80 typed A4 pages. **Hard disks** are for storing large amounts of information on and are usually used when the business has several word processing units using a **shared logic system**.

4 Peripherals

There are machines which the **CPU** needs in order to have work **input** and **output**. Examples of peripherals are the **VDU, disk drive** and **printer.**

5 Work station

The wp unit the operator sits at.

6 Stand alone system

A wp set-up with its own **peripherals.**

7 Shared resource system

Whereby several wp work stations share a resource, eg, the **printer.**

8 Shared logic system

Usually used in large establishments where several wp work stations share the **CPU** and the **printer.** These establishments would save work on to **hard disks.**

9 Main frame computer

A large business computer — unlike the **microcomputer** which you have been using.

10 K bytes

A measurement of the computer's memory — each byte is worth a unit of the computer's memory. The average A4 letter would take up approximately 2 K bytes of memory.

11 Housekeeping

The 'tidying-up' of files, ie, deleting files from disks when they are no longer required; taking copies (**back-up disks**) of files which are to be kept.

12 Boilerplating

Perhaps one of the worst pieces of jargon! This refers to taking various standard paragraphs from documents which have already been saved on to disk and then 'welding' them into a new document.

So, what will you be able to do with your word processing skill? Read on!

- INPUT TYPING — using the keyboard.

- Carry out TEXT EDITING, REVISION and REARRANGE-MENT using the commands associated with INSERTING, DELETING, CORRECTING, CENTRING, FORMATTING and JUSTIFYING TEXT (all at the touch of a button — well almost!).

- In addition the lessons cover MOVING BLOCKS OF TEXT, DOUBLE-LINE SPACING and SEARCH AND REPLACE.

- FORM INFILLING using a memo form.

- FILE MANAGEMENT — including STORAGE, RETRIEVAL, DELETION and UPDATING.

- PRINTING.

- Creating STANDARD PARAGRAPHS and STANDARD LETTERS and infilling the standard letters with VARIABLES (ie, 'personalising' the letters).

So when might you use this new skill of word processing?

For the fast and accurate typing of general business correspondence, reports and documents, but in particular for documents which may require several drafts (eg, legal documents), standard letters, standard paragraphs, form infilling (eg, invoices, 'personalising' circular letters to clients and updating directories and lists (eg, price lists).

Key to exercises

Key to section 1

Using your electric or manual typewriter how fast can you type? Thirty or forty words a minute, maybe sixty? Your speed will slow down when working on production tasks, particularly if you have to stop to correct your errors. One of the many good points about this system is that correcting errors has never been easier, whether it's just a small typing error or inserting a missing word, perhaps a whole line — or even a paragraph.

Key to section 2

To become self-employed is the aim of many people and setting up in business can change your life.

Where to start?

First of all you as the prospective entrepreneur must decide on the type of business you will establish and ask yourself is there really a market for my product? If the answer is YES then you need to decide whether you will be a sole trader or go into partnership, or form a company, perhaps with limited liability, or join with like-minded people in a co-operative venture.

Finance is, of course, of great importance and a good bank manager is essential − not only for financial advice but also for general business advice.

There are various Government initiatives to help the small business and it is important that you should be aware of the help available.

Key to section 3

BECOMING SELF-EMPLOYED

To become self-employed is the aim of many people and setting up in business can change your life.

Where to start?

First of all you as the prospective entrepreneur must decide on the type of business you will establish and ask yourself is there really a market for my product? If the answer is YES then you need to decide whether you will be a sole trader or go into partnership, or form a company, perhaps with limited liability, or join with like-minded people in a co-operative venture.

Finance is, of course, of great importance and a good bank manager is essential — not only for financial advice but also for general business advice.

Key to section 4

WORKING ABROAD

Many students are interested in working abroad once they have qualified. Some just pack-up and go with nothing in particular planned in the hope that they will find employment once they reach their destination. Others go to jobs abroad arranged through an agency in this country. However, there is another way of combining working abroad with working in London and that is with the Foreign and Commonwealth Office.

The Foreign and Commonwealth Office employs secretaries and copy typists initially to work in London for at least a year prior to being posted to a British Diplomatic Mission anywhere in the world. I know of two ex-students who joined the Foreign and Commonwealth Office and after their time in London, one went to work at the British Office in India and the other went to the British High Commission in Australia.

During their stay at their postings they both took very interesting holidays. The secretary who was sent to India, went to the exotic south of the country with its palm-fringed beaches for her holiday. The secretary who went to Australia took a trip into the inland and Northern Territories for her vacation where she saw the special magical qualities of Ayers Rock, and further north — camels, water buffalo and salt water crocodiles.

So, if you are interested in working in London and also abroad, the minimum secretarial qualifications required by the Foreign and Commonwealth Office are: 30 wpm typing for copy typist posts and 100 wpm shorthand and 30 wpm typing for secretarial posts. Positions are advertised in the national press.

Key to section 5

GOING FOR AN INTERVIEW

Are you going for an interview? Be prepared!

Find out as much as you can about the company before going to the interview and make a note of questions that you would like to ask. Make sure you know how to get to the interview address — there is nothing worse than a candidate arriving late!

Take with you items needed for a possible shorthand and typing test. If you are feeling a little nervous about this, and the typewriter is not one you have used before, ask if you can type a 'warm-up' piece first to familiarise yourself with the machine and settle yourself down.

The night before your interview re-read your copy of your application letter and curriculum vitae. Make a list of the sort of questions you would ask if you were the interviewer and then rehearse your answers. You will find that at least some of these questions will come up the next day and your answers will be ready.

As a final check before you leave for your interview make sure you take the following: the address, the name of the person you are to see and:

certificates	diplomas	notebook
pen	pencil	correction papers

84

Key to section 6

WANTED

AN EXCEPTIONAL WORD PROCESSING OPERATOR

with a minimum of 40 wpm typing who enjoys working as part of a large team in an easy-going atmosphere BUT when the pressure is on can really pull the stops out and MEET DEADLINES!

In return you will receive:

TOP SALARY
LUNCHEON VOUCHERS
4 WEEKS HOLIDAY
STAFF CONCESSIONS

INTERESTED?

Apply by (appropriate date inserted), enclosing CV and the names of 2 referees, to:

MS JANE STEVENS
PERSONNEL OFFICER
TOPS MAIL ORDER COMPANY
LONDON WC1 2XJ

Key to section 7

MEMORANDUM

FROM: Jane Stevens
          Personnel Officer

TO: Helen Jolly
          WP Supervisor

DATE: (for today)

REF: JS/SL

SUBJECT: INTERVIEWS FOR WORD PROCESSING POSITION

. . . .

To confirm our conversation of (yesterday's date inserted) concerning the 3 shortlisted applicants for the word processing position. The interviews will take place on Friday (date inserted).

The candidates are: Ms Joanna Harris, Mr John Perks and Ms Sally Holmes.

I think that it is important that they meet the staff in the Unit and see our system prior to interview. I suggest that the candidates come along to Reception at 10 am, where Sarah will meet them and bring them over to you. The first interview will then commence at 10.30 am.

Could you please confirm that this is in order, Helen.

Key to section 8

JS/SL

Date

Mr J Davies
93 Swan Street
Clapham
LONDON SW4 9PX

Dear Mr Davies

Thank you for your letter of (appropriate date inserted) enquiring about a possible vacancy in the Catering Section.

Unfortunately at the present time we do not have a vacancy. However, I will keep your letter on file and should a suitable vacancy occur in the near future I will contact you again.

May I take this opportunity of thanking you for your interest in TOPS Mail Order Company.

Yours sincerely

Jane Stevens
Personnel Officer

Key to section 9

Our Ref: JS/SL

(appropriate date inserted)

Ms J Harris
2 Kings Road
EPSOM
KT19 2PT

Dear Ms Harris

Re: WORD PROCESSING VACANCY

In connection with your application for the above post would you please attend for interview on: Friday, (appropriate date) at 10 am.

On arrival please follow the signs for the Reception Area where you will be met by Ms Lee.

I would be pleased if you would confirm whether you are able to attend as soon as possible.

Yours sincerely

Jane Stevens
Personnel Officer

Key to section 10

JS/SL

Date

Ms Sally Holmes
6 Fairway
Acton
LONDON W3 5GY

Dear Ms Holmes

RE: WORD PROCESSING POSITION

Further to your interview on (appropriate date inserted), I am pleased to inform you that you have been selected for the above position.

I am attaching two copies of your employment contract giving full details of salary, holiday entitlement, health insurance scheme, superannuation plan and staff concessions on TOPS mail order goods.

If you wish to accept this position would you please sign both copies of the contract, retain one for yourself and return the other one to me as soon as possible.

We are arranging an inservice word processing familiarisation programme so that you may adapt your skills to our system. This will take place during your first week with us.

We look forward to you commencing with us in four weeks' time on Monday, (appropriate date inserted). In the meantime, if you have any queries regarding this position please do not hesitate to contact me.

Yours sincerely

Jane Stevens
Personnel Officer

Enc

INDEX